THE RELEASE

A Collection of Poems by
Mohamed S.M. Conteh

All rights reserved and printed in the United States of America. No part of this book may be reproduced, distributed, or transmitted in any form or by any means, without the authors' prior written permission, except in the case of brief quotations embodied in critical reviews and specific other noncommercial uses permitted by copyright law.

For Publishing Information, contact Journal Joy at

Info@thejournaljoy.com.

www.thejournaljoy.com

Paperback ISBN | 978-1-957751-91-7

Ebook ISBN | 978-1-957751-92-4

Editor: Nicole Gyimah

First Paperback Edition, 2024

A Collection of Poems by

Mohamed S.M. Conteh

The Release

DEDICATION

This book is dedicated to my mother for always believing in my dreams and aspirations, and the rest of my family, for always supporting me. This book is also dedicated to those who want to dream big and execute their dreams whatever they are and for never giving up, there is not a lot of time but all we have is time, just have to make good use of time.

TABLE OF CONTENTS

LIFE

- ON TOP
- THE CHASE
- HORRIBLE DAY
- BEAUTIFUL DAY
- THE FUTURE
- BOTTOM DOWN
- THE PAST
- IN THE CAR
- THESE WIND
- STRESS BUILD
- STRESSFUL LIFE
- MAJOR PAIN
- ANOTHER DAY
- LIFE
- THE RIDE
- THIS WORLD
- THE TIDAL WAVE
- AGAIN
- ISSUES
- HERE NOW
- ADVENTURER
- DON'T WORRY

FAILURE	25
LIFE LESSONS	27
LIFE TURNS	28
LIVE LIFE	29
NAYSAYERS	30
STRONG SURVIVE	31
TIME TRACK	32
HUMAN INVASION	33
INTRODUCTION	34
10.2	35
WELCOME BACK	37
YESTERDAY AND TODAY	38
THE MAN	39
FOR ALL	40
LIFE WAYS	41
OUR LOVE	42
RELEVANCE	43
ADDICT	44
LIFE AND DEATH	45
ORIGINAL	46
PURSUIT OF HAPPINESS	**47**
LOVELY DAY	48
TIME SPEED	49
THE NEW ERA	50
INTERVENTIONS	51

- JUDGE
- MY WAY
- TALLEST PEAK
- THE HUNGER

DEATH

- PASSED
- HERE AFTER
- DIE TONIGHT

REALITY

- ITS
- THE TRUTH
- JUST BREATHE
- WATER SCRAMBLING
- TIME PAST
- INTELLIGENCE
- THE COVE
- ONE HUNDRED YEARS
- POLISH
- LIFE
- HOME HEART
- WINNER OR LOSER
- MAKE MOVES
- THE KNOWLEDGE
- LIFE STORY
- TIME FLIES

New Year 84

CITY OF VAIN 85

I STILL 87

HILLY ROAD 88

TEN 89

WATCH ME 91

LIVING IN THE PAST 92

FAST BALL 93

I AM A LABEL 95

BLUE SKY 96

THE STAGE 97

THE BATTLE 98

THOUGHTS 99

THE DEEP 100

MAKING IT 101

KNOWN 102

SATURDAY 103

MIRED 104

LOVE 106

MILY 107

FULL CIRCLE 108

THE BEST 109

FAMILY TREE 111

BONDNESS 112

BEAUTIFUL LADY 113

YOU AND I 1

CHILDHOOD 1

HOME SWEET 1

YOUNG BULL 1

INNER CHILDHOOD 1

SIERRA LEONE AKA SALONE THE BEAUTIFUL 1

ADE 1

IN DREAMS 1

OCEAN SPEAKS 1

THE BEHOLDER 1

THE STEM 1

KNOCK DOWN 1

LIKE A BIRD 1

AM I 1

EYE OPENER 1

GIVEN 1

ROYALTY 1

DREAM BIG 1

STRESS 1

INTERNAL SELF 1

THE DREAM 1

STACKING SHINE 1

THE THING 1

HIGH AFFAIRS 1

SPOKEN WORDS 1

WHY	141
DREAMER	142
SKY	143
MONSTER	144

LIFE

ON TOP

I'm on top—

I can see the whole world.

I see mountains;

From up above.

I'm flying but

I'm in control of my domain;

The reward is unrelenting.

While pursuing all options;

I don't want to touch down,

At least, not yet.

Flying like an eagle—

Destination is wherever I touchdown.

The ride of my life,

I'm on top of the world.

THE CHASE

This life is about Placement;

Its exposure to the sun.

Getting yourself ready to

Chase the dream.

The dream is filled with promise,

But promise takes hard work to fulfill;

Sometimes we persevere, but

It's keeping the faith, and

Not worrying about the naysayers.

It's going for the big dream—

It's one big chase.

The swings and the misses, to almost hitting—

And going for the jugular vein.

The impaired threshold is

Doing what's necessary;

While paying attention to the greater details.

It is what makes or breaks your dream of happening.

You have to fight for what you want.

In a meaningful and less dramatic way.

Chasing the dream happens all the time.

HORRIBLE DAY

Such a horrible day,

It makes me wonder sometimes.

Why are things the way they are?

So I beg this question.

What has been done about it?

I say life brings great challenges,

Now it's time to reflect,

And bring greater imagination.

However, it makes me wonder,

How these things have got me hovering over.

I'm looking at the next thing,

Wishful and hopeful,

But patience is a virtue.

What a horrible day!

That's how I feel sometimes.

BEAUTIFUL DAY

It is such a beautiful day,

And nature at its purest scene.

I can feel it in the air,

Like the Ninth Wonder,

Which has got me captivated,

By placing my life on cruise control.

My feet are off the pedal.

What a wonderful feeling;

As I wake up to this beautiful setting, while

Knowing that I still strive for nothing less than success.

The hunger for more and the burning desire has got me

Taking deep breaths while

Exhaling with pleasure.

I'm feeling no pressure, from the long wait at

My highest peak.

Let's go back to this beautiful day

And talk about it again.

THE FUTURE

When unsure about the future.

Taking it one day at a time,

Not knowing where this life could lead is an enigma.

Hoping for a narrow path,

Unsure about what moves to take,

Or what path that must be followed.

Unclear and uncertain at times, but only time will clear things

The story about life is written daily.

Should I feel depressed, one has to ask?

I feel that I am going through some things

If I die, how would I be remembered?

This is my moment of honesty and clarity.

Listen, I don't trust anyone

There is nowhere to go but, up and

No one to turn to, on my own

Festering through my lonely

With self-inflicted repercussion.

But that's life for you.

BOTTOM DOWN

Right from the bottom,

Looking down below

Unscattered surfaces

Rough exteriors,

About to reach base

Down but not out.

Reaching for my destination

While landing is unsmooth.

Enjoy it while it lasted

The making of this trip.

Coming from the bottom

Staying with precautions,

When I step I hear ramblings

As the earth's shakes in disbelief.

Needed to get comforted.

THE PAST

You're here now,

Why won't you forget the past

Yesterday is gone but not forgotten,

The story continues to expand piece by piece.

Watch the unraveling of it.

It could stop at any time,

But it needs to start somewhere.

Propel to reach the highest peak,

This is the mountain of luck.

As you sit back

What luck got to do with it?

It's all about self-determination and pure will;

The freshest of the kind.

It can fill up old artillery,

Hard to form, but powerful when sustained.

The grandiosity and filler when empty.

The gainer, when losing and the fight we won't lose

Not now or ever are we keeping it strong will.

The top is always hard to attain.

IN THE CAR

I'm sitting in my car,

Listening as the waves come in

This ocean speaks

It makes moves of unparalleled tides.

As I'm sitting from afar.

collecting all of my thoughts, while

Preparing this data.

So I sit back side by side

looking in all directions.

The cloud of rain evaporates,

dropping in a burst of stream.

I see the water flowing across as I sail to my destination unknown.

I bet it's heading somewhere,

Where there is peace,

Tranquility, and warmth.

I can hear the noise of the breeze

Feel it like a breeze in thin air;

It's not how it feels, but how it sounds.

What I hear is a sense of desperation, but a cool and calmness about it

That is unexplainable and sincere.

That is pure quality control,

Collectively moving in directions.

The burst of reaction is

Unmatched and un-phased

Powered by a strong will

That's genuine and sincere.

Needing its space

Now and always

So it can roam free.

I don't know where it's heading.

But it's heading somewhere.

From afar

as i sit in my car listening to the ocean

THESE WIND

Beneath these winds,

There is a deep threshold

That simmers and slithers

Beginning to slice and dice

In motion and notions.

The mind and thoughts of a closer.

Only there is opening and graving,

Willing to thread through it,

Seeing the simmering combustions.

STRESS BUILD

When stress is building up

It's the time to be active

And do things differently

What can you do differently?

Just sit back

Take some time to yourself and

Absorb some of the emotions.

Try to not lash out,

But if you do, release it carefully.

That is the right thing to do.

In the end it will be better off for you and all

Not lashing out

Just hold it,

Let it out appropriately

While keeping your sanity.

It's for the better,

I know so, since its less strain

On the mind, body and muscle.

Just feel right internally,

For no one else but you.

That is why you're doing it,

For you and no one else.

What a sigh of relief.

STRESSFUL LIFE

Life can be stressful,

Look through your rearview mirror and

Try to focus on one thing at a time, while

separating the truth from fiction

and the facts from conspiracy,

In the eye of the beholder;

Seeing is not always proof

Analyzing the subject matter first is a must,

Look through the mirror again,

What you see might be your reflection.

What you put in is what you get out.

Don't need any affirmation,

you can take it for what it's worth.

Knowing that you've created is your own domain

Don't concerned about the fallout

thus, stay even all the times

Remembering to treat life

How it should be treated.

That is, less and less and manageable stress

Each and all days.

MAJOR PAIN

Life can be a major pain,

That's if you let it be

Make it work by experience.

A true signs of endearment,

Looking for great returns.

Not putting it all in one basket.

Keeping things spaced out.

Watching every move strategically

Looking for that might be a treasure.

ANOTHER DAY

Another day has come

Another beat closer to death.

Can you feel your pulse;

Another stressful day is coming,

maybe so don't let it happen before it starts

LIFE

Another day of life;

Loving every second of it;

Breathing every scent of it;

Enjoying every breath that's taken.

I'm optimistic about the future.

This is the feel good time;

Yes, I made it my way.

I don't stress--- I'm more relaxed

I'm into life more.

I'm so grateful,

I'm never letting go.

THE RIDE

It's been one heck of a ride,

Wishing you nothing but the best

The past was just that.

Now it's time to move on from the past.

Its recreation and brand new dreams.

It's been one hell of a journey,

Can't forget the good with the bad times.

When we played and laugh hard,

With endless energy,

Like kids on a playground having fun and

Never forgetting the past.

Now plan for the future

It's been a world wind ride.

THIS WORLD

What's in the other world;

No one knows for sure.

Everyone guesses with speculatory ideation.

Trying to see what's out there;

In actuality, we really don't know;

In reality, we know what we know.

But to know what's truly out there;

We go out on a limb

With a wild idea.

Some truth and some false

I guess we will not know,

The decency of the other world.

Until we meet it, see it and grasp it

Hope it's as safe and cozy

Just like ours.

Appreciate what we do have.

Not taking it for granted;

Who really knows what's out there

Only time will tell.

THE TIDAL WAVE

I can hear the tidal wave through my ear drum

I can smells it through my nostril

When I'm by the wave its Breaths so effortlessly,

Hearing with clarity

As the water flaps

The ocean move in constant motion

Through circular current wave

Many breathe of fresh air

Its the aura of this perfect moment

AGAIN

Here we go again

Same old things.

Same old ways,

Nothing new in this world.

The more we tweaked;

The more it stays the same.

Slightly shifted,

Be careful so it don't bite you.

Don't say that you weren't warned;

You just got caught up--

In the hype.

Now you a hype person;

It's deeper than the ocean;

Watch out

You on shallow grounds,

First you must get closer.

Then you'll see;

It takes time to study.

ISSUES

Let's talk about our problems;

Let's not wait for more to compile.

Let's talk about it each day;

So we can air it out in order to move on.

Let's not wait for it to absorb;

Life is too short.

You by my arms are quite comforting.

As I rest my thoughts;

Realizing our minds as we listen to each other.

As you by my arms.

Ever so effortlessly;

Breathing a strong sigh of relief.

Saying you are not out of the woods;

Nothing burning, everything working together.

Ever so slightly;

Patience is a virtue.

As virtuous as can be.

Anything is possible,

If we're willing to work hard at it.

HERE NOW

So you here now,

Taking it one day at a time

Hanging in there;

Be brave.

Hoping things will be better,

Raise your head up high.

Be optimistic;

Looking towards the future;

Look deeper into your own eyes;

Close your eyes.

What do you see?

A brighter future,

With brighter days and calmer nights.

A sense of relief;

A new breath of fresh air.

Be strong and let nothing slow you down;

Focus on the prize ahead.

The prize of comfort;

Keep your head up and hold high.

Everything will be okay;

You just got to believe it.

ADVENTURER

Life is an adventure;

Take on the road.

The Journey of your life;

Destination unknown.

Look before you venture;

Venture into uncharted territory.

Observe carefully,

Listen very careful,

Look very closely.

Don't lose sight;

You've stayed the course.

On the road away,

Like a true adventurer.

Taking on what life brings;

Now waiting for the outcome.

Dues will be paid dividend;

From a narrow street.

That took you.

On the journey;

Of your life.

And the ride of your dream;

Road finally accomplished.

DON'T WORRY

Don't worry about Life--

Life worry for itself;

Be happy that you are living;

Worry can kill you—

It is a battlefield game; you must

Control your mental state of being, as

It controls everything.

The world is a picture

Frame by frame, being

Edited however it fits.

Everyone need to stay strong as

Destination is predetermined.

Don't provoke life, invoke it.

In a progressive world;

We need profound changes.

Kind hearted leads to compassion.

We must become leaders in order to become

A trendsetting figure.

FAILURE

Failure should never an option for you;

At times the pressure might seem quite alarming,

it mounts everyday, but

Keeping at ease all the time should always been the goal

So many temptations and

So many people don't want to see you succeed

Hoping that you fail,

But don't let that phase you.

Because phase one of failure is to

think that you are a failure,

Quickly get that out of your mind

Remember your roots and where you come from

You came from a narrow path

Coming from somewhere

From those streets of gravel bumps,

Searching for something

Thinking how you're to get up from a world of despair at times

Hope it's not too late,

If you do get up

How do you keep it up?

Life is hard,

Got to make it;

As there is no other way.

It's now, later or never;

Don't be too scared.

Or overly concerned about the times,

You've got enough to stand the test of time,

with all the weight on your back,

On tender wings

You've stood the test of time, and must keep it going.

You must pull through;

I know one thing for sure

You won't depend on no one

Win or lose

You're ready for the outcome.

Better to go down fighting; to stay afloat

better yet just stay above water

Nothing is impossible;

Or, out of the realm.

You must follow your dreams, and

Fight for what's necessary.

You're going to keep fighting

Till you can't no more.

Because failure is not an option

LIFE LESSONS

Live your life;

You living for the moment;

Day by day;

Things change all the time.

Regroup take a deep breath;

Savor your opportunities;

When it comes--

You better take charge.

It don't come very often--

Don't worry, be happy.

Get up once more and--

Shake it off,

Life's filled with obstacles.

Failure builds strong character.

If you never did, then

You'll never know.

If you never try, then

You'll never become,

Not knowing internally, for the rest of your life,

Believe in yourself;

Just as you should;

Keep living your life.

LIFE TURNS

Life has unpredictable turns--

Keep on the ride.

You are on road

Take your time,

The road can be rocky sometimes;

But, keep on the ride;

It's going somewhere.

First look where you going, and

You might hit a crossroad.

Don't worry, trust your instinct.

There will be many more bumps along.

It might take you a while,

But stick with it.

LIVE LIFE

Live life to its fullest;

You are living for tomorrow.

Knowing it's not guaranteed.

Strive to work hard;

Hope that it occurs.

Life's a big gamble;

Never knowing where you'll end up.

Take some chances;

Go against the grain;

First ask for guidance.

So you can persevere;

Under hard times,

We've all made poor choices

Numerous of times--

All we have is optimism.

When you see tomorrow,

Don't lose sight.

Knowing that,

The next day is not fully guaranteed.

Keep living your life--

You are living for tomorrow.

Keep reliving this moment daily.

NAYSAYERS

It's true what the naysayers say;

that nothing lasts forever.

Hold on to what you have;

At least temporarily.

Even if your minds gone insane,

Or you can't think clearly

You've got to get a hold of yourself,

Even if you're starting to lose it.

However, don't flinch.

Keeping it wrapped and curled under—

This life is turbulence sometimes,

So many obstacles

As you go through it's a seesaw.

The many ups and downs

You must show little fear

When the mind looms large—

Start thinking far ahead

See much further and higher than a giraffe.

You must sense danger from miles away

Your strategy should never have been to panic,

This is exactly why you should never listen to the naysayers.

STRONG SURVIVE

Only the strong make it,

No head down always looking up;

Looking for brighter days, and

The best of times.

We know some nights might be dull—

But we keep striving.

That's how life is.

And life is what you make it—

Don't hold any grudges.

Take care of yourself;

You can shine as you want to.

It takes courage, determination, and

Self-pursuit and the will to carry on.

Even though some might look at you funny

Keep your head up and look past them.

You are here for a mission

And don't let anyone in your way

TIME TRACK

Don't sleep your life away—

Time waits for no person.

Move quickly not fast,

Time never stops.

The switch stays on constantly.

Sometimes it plays slow.

Sometimes it plays fast.

So you don't stop—

Keep going and keep

Trying to be ahead of the game of life.

Falling behind will get you lost-- then

You'll never keep up with life again.

Keep up a good time.

Time never stops

So you don't stop.

HUMAN INVASION

Humans of this earth.

Who do we think we are?

We are not civilized,

We come into this planet like we own it.

Implement the rules—

Make all the changes.

Separate, divide and conquer

Enslaved the weak.

No explanation just greed—

Spoil and under civilized

That is who we are.

I just have a question;

Who do we think we are?

We will have to answer to somebody

Someday.

INTRODUCTION

Allow me to introduce myself;

My name is Mo

I grew up in a third world ghetto.

Where heroes were hard to come by;

A true adventurer from the start;

I've got no time to waste.

An explorer with far vision of a giraffe—

Created a path to walk on.

Now I'm trying to relive these dreams

A dream that is heavy.

So I'm a big dreamer heavy thinker—

That's the new movement—

Putting in work since day one.

Hoping dividend occur—

I used to be scared but now I'm brave.

Braver than a lion, feel the power.

No stopping it—

I got to the top.

But before I do;

Allow me to introduce myself again

My name is Mo

10.2

Today I narrowly escaped my death.

Nothing could have prepared me for it.

I rose up

From a tragedy bound.

Now I'm stronger.

This life won't last too long—

But I thank the man above.

For letting me see another,

And feel another breeze,

To see another light,

The essence of life;

Now I am more determined than before.

Planning to leave a mark,

One life to live,

Now it's patch work, but I've

Got to move on;

Surely but slowly.

One step at a time

with mind alertness sprinkle with greater focusness,

Body barely in tack after this day.

Thank God for that,

Happy to relieve the next disaster.

I hope to live to tell you about it.

Heads up,

no looking back.

It was already written,

This is the sequel

October second—

This day I won't ever forget.

Still got one life to protect—

I'm guiding it like a cracked egg.

stepping on the side of life

Its bruised and need patchwork—

Trying to mend my wounds.

The way that I feel,

Healing takes time to fix.

But I'm lucky to make

Another fine day.

WELCOME BACK

I came back,

Searched the soul,

Reenergize the frame.

Now a new focus,

Different mindset,

Ease into comfort ability.

In no lacks time,

Relax and ready for the future.

YESTERDAY AND TODAY

Yesterday, all my problems went away

Yesterday was the best day of my life

Yesterday, I had good food and water

Yesterday, I lost almost everything that I had.

Yesterday, my mind was at ease.

Yesterday seems so far away.

Today teaches me a lot about myself.

Today I learned not to be so mad at myself.

Today I took a stroll to the shoreline.

Today will be a day like any new experience.

Today I am looking forward to meeting some new people.

Today will be unlike any other I've encountered.

Today will not be forgotten.

Today will be a beautiful day.

Yesterday and today will forever be yesterday and today.

THE MAN

He was born to be the man

With expectation higher than the ceiling;

Talented but never practice is a recipe for failure

Skate through life thinking, how you're going to get it.

Life is all about hard work;

No room for setbacks.

The next man up is working overtime, just to be ahead.

It's harder than it ever was.

Catching up is not easy.

No room for letting up.

Being by my lonesome thinking about what this life could be.

Now it's time for recollection,

and much reconciliation.

Getting on track, working harder

Back to the fundamentals.

FOR ALL

I'm Thankful for all my experiences;

Grateful for all my sorrows

The tidal waves of up and down:

That's the trials and tribulations

that's brings our lives together

It's thrown some curveballs

Swung, missed and connected a few times;

Its taught patience;

to inspire and empower.

Loving the unfolding self more than could ever happen.

Oh, this roaring twenties

Taught more than could handle.

Its information processing,

Sometimes a ton a day,

But it's remembering how to prioritize,

You just can't this information,

Even if you want to.

Every day is development

LIFE WAYS

I gave you life;

I can take it away.

I gave you energy;

I can take that away.

I gave you strength;

I can take that away.

I gave you physical aggression;

to bring much commotion;

but I can take that away.

OUR LOVE

You are the love of my life—

I think about you all the time.

Even through the ups and downs.

I guess that's what true love is all about.

Like royalty, It was meant to last for a lifetime.

As we pass on,

Move the torch on the next, like the perfect storm.

In circular motion, like a tidal wave;

On cruise control; trying to fulfill our destiny.

It's clear that we've been impacted,

Staying afloat through rockier times will make; the love last always.

RELEVANCE

Do you want to be relevant some day;

place your passion in the correct form.

Don't worry about recognition;

That will come long after you're long gone.

Just sit back and start collecting your thoughts,

While analyzing the data

Weighing what my next move would be.

Much won't be needed,

Just enough to last comfortably.

The inspiration to keep on reaching your dreams.

You must stay focused and listen to your inner self.

It's self contagious,

Don't keep trying to be self-righteous,

So many things to tackle

I'm just starting piece by piece

Relevance is about legacy

ADDICT

An addict is someone who can't do without "the thing."

Life becomes addictive, that's why we breathe.

We let the blood pumps in our brain

It makes the air move in constant circulation.

We trained our minds to keep taking these breaths

Each one that we take becomes a cure.

Life is a medicine of itself that heals and cures

It's that point that helps us breathe accordingly.

Each time that we breathe

It heals our wounds, internally and externally.

Live it, breathe it, and take it all in

Like is truly one of a kind

It's an addictive medicine

That some might not even know

That's why I'm so addicted to it.

LIFE AND DEATH

If it comes it come

If it goes it go

When it comes I'm gone

When its gone I'm gone

It varies and it's unpredictable

Like the weather

You better get out the way

I don't want to be there

Or get there as it erupts

There is a silver lining

Either way i'll be ready

ORIGINAL

No Idea original

Everything I say has been said

Everything I did, has been done

There is nothing new to say anymore or do

My ideas were copied and traced out of someone's DNA

This DNA has some moving components

That's largely unknown

But it's living through me and soon on to someone else.

It was copied, scanned and traced.

Whatever I write down will continue to be,

The creative process and plan from other living beings.

Collectively, we continue to make a part to share

To this world as we reinvent the wheel

Again, again and again.

Ideas aren't done with originality in the first place.

No idea is original,

except for mine, of course

PURSUIT OF HAPPINESS

LOVELY DAY

This is one of those lovely days;

The sun sets up the sky;

Beaming with unheralded penetration.

The brighter of the brightest;

Sees to amaze us all

Looking through--lightning up the city;

All across town;

However-- things continue to move

In a circular motion.

Just like the earth move and

The sun penetrates, and

fills us up with clear air.

TIME SPEED

We all try to be ahead of time--

No one wants to be left aside.

Trying not to fall down--

Timing means everything.

You race against time and lose

Where many are optimistic--

The plan is to be ahead-- as you can

Never worried about time lost

be grateful about time gained.

Then you'll see it's not a joke.

THE NEW ERA

Last of an era of figuring things out;

Open to a new era.

Bigger, better and bolder;

Stronger and wiser,

The epitome of my state of mind.

Took one to three deep breaths.

And feel the depth of my society;

Walked once to hear the noise.

Looking for some correlation;

Listening to the bird speaks;

Ocean out my thoughts;

Pouring out like a river

Plethora of things on my menu.

Its deep vision and clear thinking,

Thoughts are random;

But the mission stays the same.

Always aiming for perfection,

I am forever, meticulously, brave,

To go where few people have gone.

INTERVENTIONS

In spite of these interventions;

I hold no grudges .

I made few trusted friends--

But lots of critics.

I've forgiven the betrayal, moved on

To recreate a new pack,

Now stronger than ever.

I am built to last mentally;

Whatever they say now

It's irrelevant.

I'm ahead of the pack

Older, wiser and stronger.

They can never catch me as

We are on different levels.

Now I'm hungrier for more,

My interventions are starting to pay off.

JUDGE

Don't judge me

Only God can.

My only impression is me.

I only imitate myself--

Live your life --

And let me think clearly--

You trying to be what you aren't

But you can't be me.

Don't be so judgmental--

Judge accordingly.

Stop playing a role--

Don't be a follower.

Be the leader,

People will always say--

Negative things about you and me--

They don't even know us--

Remember, before you judge--

You should ask first--

Get it from the main source.

MY WAY

I'm doing it my way

Just as I planned.

I answer to no one

Because I'm in charge.

I've seen how life works--

So I'm trying it my way.

I've got no one's help--

I will continue to make my mistakes---

But I'll show growth every time.

Now I'm doing it accordingly--

By staying strong.

A creative thinker,

Who created their own path,

Now setting a new trend;

For others to follow.

I am the master of my abilities.

TALLEST PEAK

I'm hungrier than ever to achieve my goals—

I'm stronger than ever both mental and physically

I've reached my tallest peak,

With roaring mountains just below down below

As I move close to the mountain I could see the sea levels rising up,

A jellyfish was about to sting me

I better pay attention

Or else I'm going to feel the sting

But as of right now

Im pursuing every option,

Waiting for some good news.

No time to waste—

Trying to make moves.

Before the end comes in sight.

One step at one time, I must

Follow this path and be grateful for what I have.

I've live by these principles--

Never bashful, always thankful.

Most things can be prevented--

Just know how to do it.

THE HUNGER

In spite of my interventions--

I hold no grudges.

I've forgiven the betrayal at least for now--

I'm moving on to recreate a new pack.

Staying focused on the big idea--

Keep recreating that magic.

It ain't hard to tell--

Seeing is believing.

Eyes wide open.

To see the magic.

DEATH

PASSED

Yesterday I passed,

Today's news flashed

Everyone whipped mercilessly

A story unfolds that began on its own.

As a matter of fact

Let me take you back a few decades,

To a developing story that had just begun.

I was born one hot spring day

In a heated moment

When my first exposure was to turbulence wave

It was indeed a miracle

That day was magical.

That atmosphere seemed just right.

Excited to finally come out

Flexing for more open air

Headed to a place that seems more, I thought,

Not so secluded, so I

Absorb a new air.

Seeing this beautiful new world.

Engaged in this atmosphere,

Enraged in my own domain.

From that day forward

The world would be,

According to my own viewing,

According to my own taste,

and According to my senses,

I am happy to have made it.

However, the journey has just ended

Abruptly, just as it started

Yesterday I was awaked

Yesterday I passed.

Its today news flashed

HERE AFTER

I wonder when I will go

Or how I'll die

or where I'll die

Only time will tell

For me to witness.

When I take my last breath

I hope it's deeper than

All of my thoughts combined.

Every experience I've encountered

All my trials and tribulations.

I don't really need a tribute

Hope I left earth a little easier.

Than when I arrived

So here it goes.

My last big breath

Hello to another life.

DIE TONIGHT

If I die should tonight

Don't cry for me.

Tell people I lived a full life;

The good die young.

Death comes unexpectedly;

I guess that's what life is all about,

don't take nothing for granted;

If I go, I'm pleased with how I left this earth,

Always knew that I served a purpose.

Short life span but effective,

Death has no favorites;

It needs company.

It's my time;

I was born ready;

If I should die before I wake;

Shed a couple tears for me.

Know that a soldier just died;

A fierce warrior,

Never worried about what the haters say.

If I should die before I wake,

Hold it down for me;

Shed a few more tears for me.

Matter of fact,

Savor the rest,

At least until we meet again.

Its going to be a

Cause for celebration,

Ceasing all the chaos.

At least for a day;

Live your life,

And remember me once one again

As a true hero.

REALITY

ITS

Its due diligence

Its crowded blanket and unreasonable doubt;

Its dream catcher and Captain Sea.

It's re-energized and energetic;

It's practical and pragmatic in the same realm.

Its similarity and commonality;

Its buildup refuge and soul searching.

Its breathtaking and appalling;

It's a concrete resolution and attainable re-examination.

Its focus and restless;

Its intuitiveness and stick-to-itiveness.

It's me and I.

THE TRUTH

I saw it with my own eyes

Seeing is believing but

Eyeing is optional.

See no evil, fear no evil

Live life with grace

One day at a time.

One step at a time

On time for everything.

Respecting those who respect me,

Fear none but God

The truth is what we get people to believe.

It's subjective purely in its form and interest

The truth becomes a lie and the lie is the truth

Everything comes in full motion and that's no lie.

JUST BREATHE

All you have to do is breathe,

They say one life to live.

So much to leave behind.

Last breath to take.

So much pain exuded inside of you

Vocalizing is your truest expression.

It's a lot deeper than all of us could ever have imagined

Can't fathom how you feel

Showing empathy as we begin to

Share our stories while

Reminiscing on our past.

I said hang tight as we

Pray for you.

Hoping that you make it.

We are here for support,

If you take these last breaths,

We will remember you always, regardless,

For never biting your tongue or holding your mouthpiece

A true warrior, who never cared

What's said about you

Breathe as much as you can.

When you take that last breath

We will always remember you.

As you have forever ingrained in our hearts

Known more for the good times than the bad times

Remember to breathe until you can't anymore.

WATER SCRAMBLING

Waves dancing that's my release therapy

All things racing with great laughter;

A crude inter-lude makes it a sound to be heard.

The ore of perfection is the twinkle tides;

That cleansing of abandonment is what makes life better

It's fresh like salt water,

My internal neighbor is the seeds that breathe the ocean.

It leads with attitude but yet has a soothing and calming effect.

Eyes will be closed into a dream,

Taking the imagination to great wonder.

Propel into its right senses.

The wave of signs shows

No signs of slowing down.

My mind is a lot calmer

Collecting my thoughts with ease.

That will be my release therapy.

TIME PAST

Time passed while the news flashed.

Yesterday became last week,

Tomorrow will become today.

Today will become the last month;

One month from now

Time will pass again

Forward becomes backward;

It's a seesaw wedge.

You're searching for the future, but

The future will always be the next day.

Just like yesterday was.

Haven't quite caught up to it

The past becomes the present.

Constantly moving forward

Tomorrow is the future,

As time never stops.

Tick, tock, tick, tock

Time keeps rolling

I've got to keep on rolling with time in space.

Not in a cubicle, but constantly moving forward, as

It goes on and on from afar.

Remember this,

The future is now.

INTELLIGENCE

Intelligence never sleeps.

Race against time and see who wins.

Some might say—that preparation is a must

Sleepy head never prevails,

Forward minded, and mind motion keeps all at bay.

Intelligence sleeps sometimes,

Only when necessary, but

Never absent-minded.

THE COVE

As I go deep into the cove

All I see is white streams.

Coming out my nose,

Now they are beginning to come out of my eyes.

I can't see very well

But I can manage from afar,

Eyes aren't wide shut yet.

The battle of the vision,

Now I'm in too deep,

Can't go back any more.

I'm out on my own,

Where the strong survive.

But I'm confident,

I'm going to make it.

Just not sure how,

But I have the strength to carry on,

Losing focus is not in my vocabulary.

I'm out where I can verbalize,

Taking a while to get me under

So I won't take much longer.

Like a candle about to burn.

I stay on for a while,

I've seen hell inside of me,

Now I want those good feelings again

No one has yet to survive this,

I just did survive the inevitable

My eyes are wide open.

ONE HUNDRED YEARS

One hundred years from now

What will they remember?

One hundred years from now

What will they forget?

One hundred years from now

What will be good?

One hundred years from now

What will be bad?

What are the downfalls

What are the great things?

The major failings

No ideas will go untested

Any incomplete leads to someone completion

What will we know?

One hundred years from now.

POLISH

My thoughts are polish--

My anguish is real---

I live in reality---

I can see things with clarity.

I'm patient with and unbothered

Unabashed with real consequences

Fearless and stubborn.

That's my reality--

I live it-- every second of the day

I see it every day.

I hear it every time I breathe

I read about it in my manuscript.

LIFE

Don't cry

Don't cry for end of life

Life has been one heck of a ride

Hold your tears

Tears of joy

I said don't cry

HOME HEART

Home is where the heart is

Home is where I belong

Home means everything to me

Home is too sweet

Home is relaxing

Home I can't wait to see

Home is beginning and ending

Home is about respect

Home is about power

Home needs me

Home is the same when I get there

Home is peaceful

Home is friendly

Home is Bungie street

Home is the best

Home takes it at ease

Home is the greatest

Home never forgets you

WINNER OR LOSER

Some say you got to lose before you win,

But if I lose then I'm a loser.

If I'm bad then I'm a sinner;

I say you lose then you are doomed.

I have faith in you;

Don't let yourself down if you lose;

Got to keep coming strong;

No one gives you what they want.

You must be strong will and perseverance;

That's why I pave the way for a winner.

Don't worry if you are a sinner;

In the end we are all winners;

But after we have all sinned;

The long road will seem fair;

It depends how far you go.

Many blocks come your way.

Many different paths to go;

You chose what's right for you:

Not necessarily what's best for you.

We are all living in the moment.

The present must be waited upon;

One stroke at a time.

Some might say it's genius;

I say it's repetition.

On and on until you can't no more.

In the end you win some and you lose some.

MAKE MOVES

You gotta watch your moves;

Pay close attention.

Look left and look right;

Inside out and outside in.

Traced all angles because

Everyday something is watching you;

Before you step out of your house.

To watch what you do and how you failed

You should watch what they do and learn

From their mistakes.

THE KNOWLEDGE

Thanks for all the knowledge that you gave me,

Thanks for the strength that you provided me.

Now I have the the will to carry on;

The aim is to think higher.

The guts to pursue all dreams;

Embracing all challenges;

Head on with force.

Don't know, where I am landing,

But know where I'm heading,

Watching myself.

From a third eye view;

Looking at my errors.

Trying to correct them.

All of my misfortune;

One step at a time.

That is being productive

Wild as a bull;

Contained like the temperament,

What I'm about,

Am about me,

As I hold these keys to my future.

Nothing in my past will slow me down

With the fortitude to carry myself.

The awareness to lead,

Yes I have finally arrived.

LIFE STORY

Life begins with a story

Everyday is a microcosm of the big picture

And the future of the past,

Everything goes second by seconds

Hour by hour

Day by day,

Inches by inches

Make a plan then follow.

Create your own break;

It can make or break you.

Everything is mental;

Keep your head held up.

But not too high

Never put yourself down.

Your critics will do a fine job of that for you.

Maintain by staying afloat.

Wither the ups and downs.

Your life is a story,

Help by making ways for others.

Help them succeed;

Soon they will turn on you;

It's okay, as no one is perfect.

You do what you can, when you can,

No good deeds goes bad in the long haul

Soon they will run back for more help.

Life has a funny way of playing out naturally;

Make your life interesting.

This is your story;

No one knows you better.

Do it and live it.

Watch and observe;

Don't lose sight.

Keep it within reach;

This is your path.

You are the director,

Direct it where it needs to go.

This is your life story.

TIME FLIES

They say time flies--

Only when you are having fun.

Don't have too much

Nothing good should last this long.

Keep the mind afloat.

Set your priorities straight.

Have fun but work hard, too.

All play can break you.

Free play brings some consciousness.

The ability to prosper.

Control your destiny

In the grasp of your hand.

Don't let it go,

Control and bear it.

Time is all we have,

Just use it efficiently.

Then you'll prosper wisely.

New Year

It's a new year;

A brand new day,

A new beginning,

Something to look forward to.

A clean slate.

Hoping for the best—

New things, new focus.

CITY OF VAIN

The city of vain—

Is the city of pain.

Is the city of the lost—

Is the city by the den.

Picked up and put to the side

Corruption and filled with animosity .

Unbearable damages, severely handicapped,

No one gave a damn.

The city of vain is in grave danger

All big shots are thriving—

Little men and women are being raided.

Held up against their will—

The takers are:

Egotistical and self centered,

Narcissistic and self indulgence,

The city of vain—

Is the city no one cared for,

Is the city not worth fight for

It's now worth

about two cents—

Old and worn down to its structure.

Hard to replicate—

Unlike none other

So there's no hope.

Everyone's in captive—

Escapee moved on.

To a much brighter city—

To a new city with lights

And dreams.

Which this city lacks tremendously.

Is selfless and hopeful people

The city of vain—

Is not worth talking about

Stay tuned for the conclusion

I STILL

The smoke inhalation was exasperating,

Still I breathe.

The sky was cloudy and the air was dusty,

Still I breathe.

Corruption city everyone rowdy and hard to the core,

Still I came.

Impatience drivers, horns blown and on standby, beep, beep all the time.

Still I heard.

The city in peril I just saw a thief badly beaten.

Still I watched.

The traffic is chaotic,

Couple with hours in a dreadful heat,

Still I survived.

Sweating profusely while needing a napkin

Soaked in my own hot sweat,

Heat building up like fire,

Seen so many friends, some I remembered and some I forgotten,

Still I enjoyed it.

The stay was great and the food was delicious.

That's why I came.

HILLY ROAD

That hilly road is--

Way too dangerous.

Only a few have made it count.

Cars come and go,

But only a few survive it.

That hilly road,

The most dangerous of them all.

That hilly road,

Not to be played with.

It will leave you

On the road.

For days.

TEN

When I was ten years old,

I stayed out past my curfew.

Running home from the streets,

You would think that I was being chased by someone.

Came home everyone fast asleep;

Sneaked through the back door,

Tippy toed my way to the room

About to open the door,

Found out, the room door was locked and secured.

The living room was dark as hell,

I can't seem to find this handle.

Asking myself:

Where is the door handle?

Finally I found the door handle.

About to open the door,

Forced myself into the bed.

As I went under these blankets, I

Tucked myself in,

Snoring like a baby

Woke up the next morning,

This all happened one memorable night, and I

Said to myself "no more missed curfew."

This all happened

When I was ten years old.

WATCH ME

Watch me make something out of nothing.

Turn nothing into something.

Split scene with me on both side

It's the good minus the bad.

Things never the same,

But more or less the same.

It's keeping the sanity and sanctity,

Nonetheless becomes nevertheless

Heard "what's been said!"

Produce the reproduction,

Increasing the liveliness,

Build on what's effective—

Carry out like a trace.

Repeated but never duplicated

Its different beats for different hearts.

Eaten like a piece of bread, Swollen then digested,

Repeated for clarity and elaborate for those interested.

Seeing others point of view, while looking from my own peripheral standpoint.

The future is handed to me,

But nothing like a silver platter, that's

Waiting to be served.

I suggest you watch me, too.

LIVING IN THE PAST

Living in the past,

When things are glistered

And mightier, the best of times,

The testament of recent times.

Where worrying was so much less

Everything can be quite handy.

Looking forward to the future,

By taking it one step at a time.

Hour by the hour,

Enjoying the moment.

Just like yesterday.

No bitterness,

Pure joy.

Engraved into the moment,

When it is gone.

Living in the past,

Like dinosaurs ruling this earth.

Way beyond our imagination.

Living in the past,

The best experience is the last.

Things that you could never get back.

Thankfully it was in the past.

FAST BALL

Today I dodged one,

Came down live last a fast ball

But, livelier than the era ever was;

Landed with bruising scars.

Now am ready to come up with force.

Recharge the mind and handle with ease.

A chance to rekindle some things in the mind

I am hopeful for what this experience brings.

I hope that it brings growth and maturity.

Where destination is not too far ahead

I am looking through the tunnel.

Eyes gleaming through the light

seeing what this obstacle brings.

Experiencing is believing;

Nothing beats firsthand knowledge.

Or nothing beats what's seen;

I'm now able to see the trend.

I was able to seek: the outcome,

the pain and the aggression.

While looking at myself.

I got a lot to say and lose

A collection of thoughts and units

I'm informed about the precursor,

Now I've got my mind right.

It certainly was not that easy

Got a glimpse of what this is all about;
for that I'm a better person.

Right the second I am.

Then I'm gone to my humanly ways.

Each experience is fresh and daily.

Tomorrow I might dodge a new one.

Let's see what happens next.

I AM A LABEL

I am defined by my peers.

I am defined by my income.

I am defined by my critics.

I am defined more than once.

I am defined by my teachers.

I am defined by my mentors

I am defined by my nemesis.

I am defined by my friends.

I am defined by my family.

I am defined by what I don't have.

I am defined for who I am.

I am defined by my people.

I am defined for myself.

I am defined by you.

I am defined by me.

I am just a label

BLUE SKY

The sky is blue

The stars are shining.

The trees are different

The earth is round.

People think differently, with

No two things are the same.

No matter how you slice or dice it.

Some will get this others won't

We are all one big melting pot

Out to stir in our direction—

To a place where it's comfortable—

To a home where there is no pressure.

No worries or trouble.

Living carefree with no rules.

The sky is blue, according to him;

The sky may be a spot of white or gray;

According to him,

We are all so different; yet, so the same.

THE STAGE

We are all in this great stage,

Some of us famous,

While some of us are nameless.

Some of us will fake it,

Until we make it.

Some of us will breakthrough

And some of us will be waiting.

For that day may never come through.

Some of us are bold;

While some of us are hesitant.

Some may be cowards;

Some of us are appalled.

Everyone watched closely;

Some will be anointed.

Some will be deserted;

It's the luck of the draw—

The odds might go away,

One thing for certain,

You got to go and get it.

THE BATTLE

Today I lost a war

But the battle has just begun

Now Its time to go back and reshuffle.

Time to recharge and re-strategize

From a broader lenses.

Just got to look deeper

Into the ocean.

With careful proclamation, and

Much careful preparation.

The gamble was lost, but

No time for foolish betting.

I've got to tighten my belt.

with nothing to lose, not even a drop of a dime.

From here on it's just cause

No more lost war

The greater gain

With higher authority

And selfless power

Poise under pressure.

THOUGHTS

Remember me for the good and the bad times

Know that I'm not perfect,

even though I tried to be.

I fell short of it many times,

it's quite painful just awful

Thriving and surviving in this world filled with jealousy and greed

Know that I channel all my knowledge for the good

Of the people never made excuse

I just play the cards I'm dealt with

I could have complain but no one got the time and patient to hear me out

So I keep on keeping on like a straight arrow.

THE DEEP

This is deeper than the ocean

Layers of bricks higher than the Himalayas

Thoughts bigger than the grand canyon

What's been scribble is used solely for artistry purposes

So I can show you what I'm about

The true testament

Of poetry

I don't tell lies, just actually stories

MAKING IT

Will I make it

Will I break free

I told you'll

That I'm going to make it

Time is of the essence

I won't stop

I'll keep going strong and hard

Until I make it

It's awful timely

No sincere apology

Just plain confident

And the right competency

The right moves

I know I will make it.

KNOWN

If I were to be known

I would want my face etched in carnelian stone

So I can be seen across the globe

I want it traced on construction paper

Making everyone recollect and wanting a piece of my head

In essence all I ever cared about is me

If I were rich, if I were known, if I were still alive

I'll have all my worth spewed in crystal white sand

It will begin to peel as an onion

With each level to the core

Then and only then

Would I be known.

SATURDAY

Every Saturday I sit my entire body down

To gravitate then meditate

Legs crossed and feet up high like the ceiling

It takes complete concentration

The wither of all that good

I'm in my comfort zone

Just relaxing, then meditate some more

My phone's on silent

A tradition like none other

When I sit, I don't move a muscle, unless I have to

I don't reach for nothing unless I have to

Because it's the thing to do

Every Saturday is when I watch college football

In front of my living room

With my eyes wide open.

MIRED

Nothing else matters to me

But my full and undivided attention

So I can retain and grasp

To hold on for decades to come

At least until i am old, fat and bald

Until I see no more gray

That will be the day

They way i am describing myself

You would think

I'm some egotistical

Self centered, narcissistic pre-Madonna.

When in reality

I'm just trying to be;

Sheltered like that young child who plays piano for the first time

That feeling of timid and tenderness arises

But with time and experience all things would be found out correctly

You see, this won't be the only thing I'm focused on

There will be much more

Each has its own patterns and trends

And no one involved but me

I'm in my worlds because all I see is I

Nothing else matters to me as once alluded

My focus runs deeps

One track at a time

LOVE

Love is beauty

In the eyes of the beholder

It peaks from the tallest mountains

From far above the Rockies dwell

It is corral by its taste

Which gets carried like pedestals.

The eyes of the beholder

Seeks to find refuge, purity and sensibility

What beauty becomes is love that's genuine

To love is to engage.

To seek is to cherish beauty

Which becomes an act of endearment

FAMILY

FULL CIRCLE

Everything comes in full circle,

My family is a real dynasty.

Strong-willed through thick and thin

We are strong willed, so we perseverance;

Through hard times

I'm the umbrella that stirs the melting pot.

It's what melts that keeps us afloat.

Although I feel the perfect storm coming,

In unwavering compulsions

No worries,

I don't sink, I swim harder and wiser.

Enough to keep all heads above water.

THE BEST

Wishing you nothing but the best

But don't forget about the past

It's been a blast,

While we still got time

Let's party and have fun

We're still young anyways

Enjoy the sunshine;

As we gazed our eyes at the wind,

While we stir at the sun with our naked eyeballs

We both fell and got right up.

Now it's a new focus

Stronger and better.

Concentration with full force,

So much to look forward to and

No worries, just pure joy.

In this sea of light

Clearing up in the sky,

Like a light with extra ray,

Beaming with high penetration---

Now hope floats---

The immaculate one-- no wonders

Tethering from one to the other

From a promised new hope--

With new beginning and understanding

Let's hope and have less fear

Within ourselves---

Can't evade it---

But hoping to mitigate it.

FAMILY TREE

The family trees that bond like one--

Like a butterfly flying through with ease

Sizing up all our opportunities

Filled with peace and serenity;

The will to keep on and exude pressure

Holding on and never letting go,

Focused and strong will,

Exceeding all expectations

Worry free and stress less

That's our family tree.

BONDNESS

We were meant for each other--

Built by an everlasting bond.

That makes us inseparable

Only time will tell

The test that we will face.

We were meant to be.

We are inseparable link—

Tied together like a chain.

We'll have stood the test of time.

BEAUTIFUL LADY

Sounds coming from a far—

Putting ears to the phone.

Doesn't seem that far

Its that magic tune

That stays connected

Hearing all the wealth of acknowledgement.

Knowing that it's mutually connected—

Reciprocal from both ends.

And a greater understanding

And appreciation, that's agreed upon by all.

With great pleasure and aptitude

No guilty verdict

But predictable outcome.

That goes farther while coming from a far.

I'm sitting and listening on the telephone.

Wishing you were next to me,

the soundwave through the phone;

Only we are interconnected—

With clarity and patience.

I've never felt this comfortable—

Until I spoke to you, beautiful lady.

YOU AND I

You and I

Were meant to be

You and I

Were meant to last

You and I

Will have to be

You and I

Were meant to be

You and I

Are on the prowl

You and I

It's just you and I

CHILDHOOD

HOME SWEET

They say home is where the heart is

So I left only to return

Like it was yesterday.

I left home so many years ago

I recently came back from many miles away

Across a large sea.

I always remember home for those quiet nights,

It's like my mind never left.

Home is truly special to me,

It's the beginning of my upbringing

I'm so thankful for home.

I wish I could stay longer

But now I've got a new focus.

Trying to one day make it better.

First I must learn new skills

Bring them where it all began.

Make my home more powerful

Empower my people

To be leaders.

Home is truly special to me.

That is why I could never forget

Where my home is.

YOUNG BULL

I was raised as a young boy,

In a city called Freetown.

In a country named Sierra Leone.

By near a street called Bungie,

In a town called Fourah Bay,

Went to a tiny school,

Yet it was so remarkable

One of the best experience I ever had

The people were intelligent

And everyone had one big ego.

But we were like a family

Sierra Leone is my home

Freetown is my city.

Fourah bay is my town.

Bungie Street, is my neighborhood

Now I can go home and just relax

And reminisce like the young bull I was

INNER CHILDHOOD

Somebody wake me I'm dreaming

Visions of impairments, which

Started as a youth.

Channeling thoughts of a grown-up

Young and ambitious

The mind of a teenager—

Alert looming and scheming.

Wondering, what is this?

Youthful mind and youthful soul

Don't know why but

Thought started pouring out.

Like a storm, without letting off.

The gift I retained

Are knowledgeable skills.

Hard to express at first, but

The first wasn't the last.

The last never came—

Like the first didn't want to come.

The mind of a youngster.

SIERRA LEONE AKA SALONE THE BEAUTIFUL

Salone, where all my troubles seemed so far away.

A place where I could just relax, call home and recollect

Salone, where my humble beginnings come from

And humility came about.

Oh Salone, the beautiful

I still believe in you.

ADE

Ade was the best runner in school;

No one could get any closer.

He out-ran all of his competitors.

Blew each out of the water; and

Most importantly, Held the team together

Once he has the baton,

He flew like a jet.

Ade was, a wild boy on the streets,

With a sense of desperation,

Running like he had no sense.

That's about all he knew.

But he was the best there was

The mightiest of them all,

And the fastest.

Faster than a changing street light going from yellow to red.

I will always remember Ade

IN DREAMS

OCEAN SPEAKS

I'm listening to the ocean

As my thoughts reappear.

Over and over

As my mind regains its form

I have the mind and the will to carry on to this world

As I face up to my nemesis,

I speak softly but carry a lot of depth

From that I'm stronger,

Could not do no wrong

In spite of my limitations

I don't vex,

On an intellectual level

I've got a creative mind.

Watch as I keep hope alive

The prophecy leads by doing,

No angel, but I live vicariously

Leader of the pack,

I'm a one-man band that

listens to the ocean.

When my thoughts pour,

I'm beginning to feel this commotion.

My mind reappears again

Guided by a streaking light;

Halted by the screeching wind.

Waterfalls drop back and forth

The mind of this twirling wind.

THE BEHOLDER

The eye of the beholder;

A toothless creature.

Which cannot speak,

But it sees, hear, and observes

It takes correct notes.

Learning to express it well.

In another fashionable way,

Who is this creature?

One will never know,

Truth be told,

It's an imaginary eye,

So do not forsake it,

Or, what this creature possesses?

The truth shall remain,

In it eyes, of course.

THE STEM

The rose that stood on its stem;

The fresh scent which smeared all around us

It leaves a twinkle in one's eyes.

Itching to be scratched

Wipe down with one tissue

It appears to tears that will never fall off,

Reminisces of the happening

That joy of flamboyant route and

The fixture of expulsion

With sincerity like a rose standing

KNOCK DOWN

Knock, knock, who is there--

I'm not too sure but don't want to open.

The door was stuck,

It was early one morning

Barely slept, I swear it was the longest night ever.

Young, focused, but still

Not answering the door.

The noise uttered my name---

Who could that be? 'I said"

I ponder to myself as

I must take cover.

Is this a dream or is this really going on?

The thumping and loud sound increase one notch higher;

Reluctance to open not knowing, who it could be

Already made up my mind not to open

the door, the voice said

my name one more time.

The door was jammed

So it would have to be forced--

To get open,

But i'm hanging in there--

And ready for what happens

Someone about to step in.

Got my club in my hand,

Just ready to defend--

Here it goes, knock again

The door opened and I clipped some in their face.

Door they go, as I unveil this mask—

Little did I know it was a young man who's lost.

Who wanted to scare me, but he got dethroned

In the head, and now he is down.

And cannot get up.

Knock Knock I am here

LIKE A BIRD

If I could fly like a bird

I'll be in the air in its purest form

I would be "Gone with the wind"

While elevated from the bottom to the very top

Peripheral view from the air up top.

I stand high like the mountain

Eyes wide open like an eagle

I can see all and reach most

That's why I want to fly like a bird

AM I

Where am I?

Or, where am I going?

I'm asleep; I can't wake up.

I'm entering a world of indulgence;

All I see is the star.

When do I wake up?

this seems interesting

Wake me up,

I can't get up;

It's a sick dream.

Or Is it reality?

Or, Is it a dream?

EYE OPENER

I don't know how to sleep;

So I stand on my toes.

Those that pray for my downfall,

Can forget about it.

They say you snooze, you lose,

So If I sleep, I'm losing.

For fear of a rude awakening;

I've got one eye open.

Eyeing my next move,

Ready to take whatever this life brings,

One eye at a time.

Theses eyes never shut

I'll eventually sleep when I die.

GIVEN

I've been blessed to

Wake up each morning

To good health.

Happy to be here and

Glad to be alive.

Reason with a cause,

Thrust upon my well being--

Way beyond my imagination.

I've got an eye out---

Looking to guide me--

I'm following their lead--

Asking for protection.

To take me somewhere;

To a place that I don't know.

Hoping for a smooth landing

Knowing full well nothing goes smoothly

But I'm an optimistic--

The good comes with the bad sometimes

They are tied in relative form--

But I'm patiently waiting--

For the outcome I will get.

ROYALTY

One of a kind—

Since I just hit the lotto.

I made the royal flush, then I

Hit the jackpot.

I'm feeling like royalty these days.

It's something magical and special.

I did something that only happens one in a trillion

It's nothing quite like it.

That's a known fact.

Got any questions.

You should ask about it.

This can't be real—

Woke up this morning.

It was all a dream,

I'm a big dreamer.

There are two realities.

I like the dream better,

But reality is a struggle.

But I'm making the best of it.

DREAM BIG

If you're a big dreamer,

And are slightly delusional about fame,

you've got to remember that fame brings unwarranted problems

and deeply seated unresolved issues.

You've got to realize that this isn't a game but rather life on a game.

Nonetheless, strive and thrive under pressure.

Being on survival mode won't last—

It's not a blueprint for what success is all about.

If you're trying to reach the highest peak

Remember to always reach for the sky

Some might say it's impossible.

You say, "sure I can't get it all in one massive take,"

But nothing has ever stopped you from trying

Reaching that conquest is, What you're all about.

You see the big picture, in your rear view mirror

Lenses are a bit out of focus, but always focus.

Clear on what you want, and counting on the outcome.

You're about to make this dream,

A reality from your imagination.

STRESS

Eat, sleep, stress, work, tool, die--

Hallucinate, dream fantasize, awake, oh reality.

Lost one, lost two, lost many, finally drew.

Looking and can't find, ask the kids?

Keys hiding got to dig deeper.

Searching and looking for something--

I found that and now I'm relieved.

Who would have thought?

Many problems—

Yet so few solutions.

INTERNAL SELF

I am sitting next to you—

So you can see what you can become.

I 'm sitting next to you—

So you can listen to what you can become.

I am close to you—

So you can breathe sense and hear about you.

This is your life—

Face to face to you.

This is what you can expect,

If you follow through.

THE DREAM

We are all in multiple

Layers of dream.

With each one being created

Each and everyday of our lives.

When we cannot dream,

Then we cannot imagine,

Then we cannot see,

And then we cannot hear.

A dream within a dream

STACKING SHINE

Stacking me shine--

Traveling round the world.

Seeing many faces, while being in a relationship with many people.

Some old and some young--

Remember many

But I missed a few.

Memory is applauded,

No questions about it.

Things are the way they were.

Years later still, things are

Through a period of abandonment.

Or is it a period of no resourcefulness.

Things stayed the same,

Exactly alike.

No modes for repair,

No reconciliation

It just is,

And its accepted.

Done in deliberation.

THE THING

What to do?

Where to turn?

When to run?

Escaping this reality brings

Sadness and grief.

Great upstart optimism.

The other end of it;

The pressure cooker.

Mind guessing;

Alarm still floating.

HIGH AFFAIRS

High affairs mixed with high drama—

In a street, where

You are cornered.

No room to breathe, it's all high stakes.

Mixed with high pressure and alertness.

Quite weary about the next foe.

Where each step is calculated.

And each move is microscopic,

Of how things really are.

Nowhere to run and hide

In stalemate mode.

eyes wide open--

Can't see very near. but

Can dream far away places.

This is,

High affairs in ruins.

SPOKEN WORDS

Interest sparks motivation, but behold that daunting task.

Encourage those who are learning more as they are yearning for success.

Patience is a mindful game, just play it how you read it

Selection is all about excitement,

Evaluating the successes is an easy task.

A Spoken word is a very powerful tool

to use, and adhere by.

WHY

Why is he here?

He ponders the question.

With no real answer, I see why.

He was blessed with skills

Talent that will take him somewhere.

Watch as he brace the optimist,

And shiver pessimistically.

He has been sent for a battle.

Like most he has been battle tested.

Not one to worry about critic—

Going out his way and not letting up.

Next time you asked go ahead, but remember

One thing, one question;

Why.

DREAMER

Imagine if I stop dreaming

That would be the end of me

I would be dead and buried six feet under

I'll be like an old soul

Filled with rust and maggots covering my skin

Imagine if I stop dreaming

I would be buried dead or alive

Deep into the gravel's dirt

Drugged up and replaced by some new dead blood

After centuries of sleepless day and night.

Dirt covering my face with molds and bugs

I would be scooped up and left atoned for my own corpses

I'm a dreamer who dreams whether dead or alive

SKY

I am the antithesis of the sky

I siphon through the moon

Looking to show face

My intent is to glide through

To a far away land

Only to be seen again

In another galaxy

Brief and consciously

MONSTER

With its long beak and flimsy feathers

The evilness seeks inside of it

Long legged, heavy chested, long winded on the prowl

Attack minded and vicious as can be

It presents lingering effects and gigantic exteriors

With shorter attention span

It puts up with no bull

Defensive minded, toes curled up like a newborn baby

Stomping all over with force

Its eyes gazes tormenting in despair

Long winded slow to get up

Once up, on the go with fearless attitude

Makes everyone around

Feels its glaring presence

This monster is beautiful and ferocious

Printed in the USA
CPSIA information can be obtained
at www.ICGtesting.com
LVHW090236091024
793326LV00002B/260